An Introduction to
Fashion Illustration

Madeleine Ginsburg

Assistant Keeper, Department of Textiles and Dress
Victoria & Albert Museum

V & A / Compton / Pitman

Copyright © Madeleine Ginsburg 1980
First jointly published in Great Britain in 1980
by The Compton Press Ltd., 53 Pound Street,
Warminster, Wiltshire and
Pitman Publishing Ltd., 39 Parker Street,
London WC2B 5PD.

Designed by Humphrey Stone and
edited by Anthony Burton
Printed in Great Britain by
W. S. Cowell Limited, Ipswich
ISBN 0 273 01471 4

To L.B.G. *with affection and gratitude*

ACKNOWLEDGEMENTS

I acknowledge with thanks the contributions made to
this book by Jean Hamilton, Department of Prints,
Drawings and Photographs, Victoria and Albert
Museum, Hélène Alexander, Lindsay Stainton, Depart-
ment of Prints and Drawings, British Museum, L.
Dethan and F. M. Rocket of the French Section,
British Library, also to M. L. Richards and David
Levy.

   My thanks are also due to Charles Gibbs Smith,
John L. Nevinson, and the late James Laver for advice
and encouragement over the years.

Introduction

Fashion plates have always been 'arch persuaders', and it is a tribute to their charm, transcending the clothes which we now find funny or foolish, that they have such enduring appeal. Baudelaire saw in their trim little figures images of human perfectibility, but this may be too elevating and challenging a concept for most of us, who find in them only nostalgia and escapism. They are like a personalised social history or, as one of the great 18th-century publishers called it, 'l'histoire morale'. Above all, they tell the story of clothes visually and precisely, and we have summarised it in our choice of illustrations.

They also represent an aspect of the media, for they are part of the development of the fashion industry, showing people what they should wear. The late James Laver, pioneer historian of the subject, has commented that in modern times they dealt in prophecy as opposed to an earlier age when they were concerned with rapportage. It is in that earlier age that their origins lie, in the pictures of clothes and peoples of all nations which the engravers of the 16th century provided for those who wished to know more about their suddenly expanding world.

In the 17th century, perhaps significantly an age which saw the birth of the social contract, interest shifted to clothes indicative of class and occupation and engravers depicted the nobility as being synonymous with 'La Mode'. Even when fashions were divorced from personal and social connotations, as they began to be towards the end of the 17th century, and were valued for their own sake, fashion plates were still rapportage. It was only in the last quarter of the 18th century, when a sophisticated dress-obsessed public had exhausted the variety available to them and demanded novelty, that there were signs of change, and during the 19th century this trend was intensified by commercial pressures within the clothing industry to foresee and even shape future demand. It was confirmed when fashion designs became recognised and appreciated as valid works of creation.

As works of art, dress and fashion plates are usually classified under the heading 'Illustration', and during their four hundred years of history they demonstrate techniques and reflect trends common to all branches of the subject. They have been produced by artists of repute though it must be admitted sometimes anonymously and reluctantly as a bread-and-butter chore. The results do not necessarily suffer and there are some artists who have responded superbly to the challenge of depicting clothes and fashions, raising them to the level of minor masterpieces.

The early illustrated costume books from the 16th century are known as Trachtenbücher, the German 'Tracht' meaning clothing. For the most part their text is minimal, sometimes but not always serving to identify the plates showing figures wearing the clothes peculiar to their nationality or rank. There is sometimes an historical prologue, vague and generalised in character, usually more precise and representative within the period of the living memory of the artist. Fantasy fills any gaps in the sequence. Since titles are repetitive variations on the same theme – the clothes and peoples of the world – the books are usually referred to by the name of the author – though possibly compiler would be a better word, for they tend to be rather derivative. To judge by the number of titles and editions they were popular, and a certain degree of repetition is to be expected when demand puts pressure on the supply of original material. People were avid to know more about strange clothes and customs, indeed they still are, but in the 16th century travel was difficult and resources very limited. The compilers may have exploited the gullibility of their readers but they did not necessarily take it for granted. Deserpz, who wrote the introduction to one of the earliest Trachtenbücher in 1563, reassures his readers that 'le tout fait après le naturel', and gives credits for the information to the late Captain Roberval, a traveller, and 'un certain Portugais': a country famous for its explorers at this time.

On the whole it is reasonable to suppose that the engraver is most reliable when he is nearest to home, like Jost Amman on the dress distinctions of the various German city states, and the Bertelli family on those of Italy, but critical analysis is easier if the editions are taken in chronological order and there is an excellent recent concordance.

English dress makes a solitary and not very enlightening appearance in François Deserpz's *Recueil de la diversité des habits . . .* (1st ed. 1563). It does not appear among Enea Vico's large clear engravings nor in their more accessible reversed copies by Ferdinando Bertelli. It is best seen in Abraham de Bruyn's *Omnium Poene Gentium* (1st ed. 1577), copied successively and much less clearly in Pietro Bertelli's *Diversarum Nationum Habitus . . .* (1st ed. 1589) and in Alexandro Fabri's *Diversarum Nationum Ornatus* (1593).

A new dimension is added to this type of publication when Donato Bertelli in *Le vere imagini et descritione delle piu nobilli città. . . .* (1569) and Pietro Bertelli in his *Diversarum Nationum Habitus* add pull-up flaps to some of their pictures, especially those where ladies' legs, as shocking to the 16th century as to the 19th, were of importance. The combination of polite porn and toy book, packaged as general education, must have been irresistible.

Only in Cesare Vecellio's (1521–1601) *Degli Habiti antichi et moderni . . .* (1st ed. 1590, 2nd ed. 1598) do the pictures by Christoph Krieger have less interest than the text. This shows an unexpected talent as writer in Vecellio who was Titian's cousin and assistant. Age did not dim the author's enthusiasm for the subject and each of the texts impresses on its own merits. The earlier one is more anecdotal, valuable for its comments on the way in which the book was compiled. He tells of correspondence with Master Erasmo Falte, court librarian of Parma, about the distinctive dress of that city, and of pictures sent to clarify information. He has the artist's eye for colour and detail: who else would mention that the noblémen of France wear their hose so short and tight that they show the veins on their thighs? He is also helpful when he commends the wares of Master Bartolomeo Bontempele, silk merchant, at the Sign of the Chalice in Venice, here almost edging into the modern world of fashion linked with commerce.

Trachtenbücher continued to be compiled well into the 18th century, but towards the end they lost their novelty and their quality diminished. With few exceptions the later ones are little more than random collections of crude re-engravings from other people's originals.

In the hands of Abraham Bosse and Jacques Callot engraving became a social record, and the latter's studies of the nobles of Lorraine (1624), are said to have inspired Bosse's engravings after Saint-Igny, *La Noblesse françoise à l'Eglise* (1624) and his *Le Jardin de la Noblesse.* All show well-dressed figures posed theatrically, for the most part alone against a minimal but effective landscape. Bosse, perhaps because he was the son of a master tailor, seems interested in clothes almost for their own sake. His plates *Before and After the Edict* (1633) show a fashionable lady and gentleman as they were affected by Richelieu's Sumptuary Law: with and without the prohibited luxuries of lace braid and embroidery. His *La Galerie du Palais* (1636), the booths of this fashionable shopping place stocked with minutely detailed accessories, collars, cuffs, ribbons and fans as well as the clothes of the shoppers, suggests that as a restraint on extravagance the Law may not have been very effective. Not all his work is dated, but it spans the 1630s and 1640s and shows the short-waisted rounded styles changing to a longer-waisted straight cut line. He illustrates all aspects of contemporary French life at its most well ordered, and shows clothes realistically modified by rank and occupation against carefully observed backgrounds.

English women are to be seen in the work of Wenceslaus Hollar (1607–77). He was born in Bohemia and studied engraving in the Netherlands, entering the household of Thomas Howard, Earl of Arundel, during the mission to Vienna in 1635. Except for a short period during the Civil War he was to remain in England for the rest of his life. He worked in all branches of his craft but he is best known for his topographical work and for his realistic and finely detailed pictures of women. The *Ornatus Muliebris or the Severall Habits of English women from the Nobilitie to the Country Women as they are at these times*, a series of twenty-six plates published in 1640, achieves exactly what it sets out to do and provides a picture of women of all classes, including back as well as front views. With the *Theatrum Mulierum* (1643), a set of forty-eight engravings later augmented to a hundred and published in 1646 as 'Aula Veneris', he turns to a wider theme and provides what is almost a feminist Trachtenbuch largely based on original material, sketches that he must have made during his travels in Europe. Some of his decorative pieces may be emblematic, like 'The Seasons', but they are still consciously realistic. They were drawn from life or else copied from one of his earlier originals. Their dress was modified according to the temperature: in Winter they were snug in hood, mask and muff, while in Summer their faces were shielded with veils and their shoulders were bared to the sun. Those with recognizable London backgrounds were particularly popular and were copied by others without significant alteration as late as the 1650s.

Accessories of 1647: muffs, collars, masks, fans and gloves.
Etching by Wenceslaus Hollar, 1647.

Despite their small scale and static pose, Hollar's like-nesses of women have an affecting and surely affectionate realism. John Aubrey, the 17th-century biographer who knew and liked him well, wrote that he married a waiting woman of the Earl of Arundel and that he had a daughter, 'that was one of the greatest Beauties I have seen'. He also mentions Hollar's extreme short sight, though it was obviously no bar to a keen observation of the feminine world around him. It may even have been an advantage, for those close-up views of accessories, furs, fans, collars and gloves, are '*tours de force*' of texture.

Despite, or perhaps because of, political tensions and social upheaval, men's fashions during the mid 17th century became so extreme as to cause considerable inconvenience to their wearers. The significance of the remedy, the introduction of the long semi-fitted coat which reduced abbreviated doublet and wide saggy hose to a new status as undergarments, was perfectly apparent to contemporaries and aroused comment in both England and France. Sebastien Le Clerc (1637–1714) includes a figure in doublet and petticoat breeches, and another wearing a long coat, in his small un-captioned and retrospective series, *Divers Costumes Francais de la Regne de Louis XIV*, and both styles are also to be found in Raymond de Hooge's *Figures*

à la Mode, undated, though they have been assigned to his Paris period, after 1662. The ladies and gentlemen, one or two to a plate, are shown against a distant but detailed background, their foreshortened fashion plate proportions emphasising the line of their clothes. This was a new device and rarely used again until the late 19th century. The men loom with an elegant menace which effectively negates any suggestion of effeminacy caused by the copious ribbon trimmings or skirt-like breeches.

During the reign of Louis XIV France began to consolidate her role as international leader of fashion. Jean Baptiste Colbert, the minister of Finance, em-barked on a systematic development of the luxury trades and the court of the young Roi Soleil, rife with competitive ostentation, became a model for Europe. It was the confirmation of an already existing trend and, as John Evelyn shrewdly observed in *Tyrannus or La Mode* (1661), fashion changes in France could be construed as policy rather than frivolity: 'It is plainly in their interest and they gain by it. Believe it, La Mode de France is one of the best returns they make, and feeds as many bellies as it clothes backs.'

Despite this stimulus, obtaining news of new fashions remained a matter for individual enterprise, reliance on

5

observers, well-placed agents and correspondents. The main burden seems to have fallen on the fragile shoulders of the fashion dolls, miniature mannequins commissioned from milliners and dressmakers. There are references to these dolls dating from the 14th century. They were good for showing details of cut but they were expensive, delicate and difficult to transport.

It was not until 1672 that a systematic and pro-professional attempt was made to provide news of the latest fashions. Journals were a male preserve concerned mainly with war and politics until Jean Donneau de Vizé, a not too successful dramatist, founded *Le Mercure Galant*. This was aimed at a leisured and general readership and included fashion among the subjects that it covered, though it was not until 1678, after its re-organisation as *Le Nouveau Mercure Galant*, that there appeared a series of articles accompanied by fully-captioned illustrations together with the addresses of some suppliers. This was the first fashion coverage on modern lines, though it lasted no more than that one year. It gave precise details of winter clothing for a courtier in full dress, a gentleman in outdoor dress and a lady in formal and informal dress. Later in the year the June number showed suitable summer dress for a lady and a gentleman and the October number showed winter fashions. The greatest change was to be seen in the ladies' dress – now a loose-fitting overgown worn over a corset and petticoat had replaced the boned stiff-bodied gown depicted by de Hooge.

The interior of a Paris milliner's shop issued with the *extraordinaire* (special number) of 18th March showed accessories and fabrics in great detail and discussed them in the text, together with Donneau de Vizé's printed request for samples, figures habillées or drawings for reproduction in the magazine. Thereafter the coverage lapsed and there were no further illustrated fashion articles in the Journal until its re-appearance as *Mercure de France* in 1729.

Part of the reason for this may have been the increasing abundance of large-scale decorative popular prints in line and possibly in colour. Their subjects varied and included royal and popular personalities, decorative and emblematic figures as well as illustrations of new styles. Whoever or whatever was portrayed in these plates was always in fashionable dress; it was this characteristic that gave them the colloquial term, *Les Modes*.

The prints were the work of the Bonnarts, the St Jean and the Arnoult families, among others. Being signed, captioned and dated they are most useful charts of the change towards increasing sobriety and formality of dress during the last sad years of the reign of Louis XIV. The retrospective sets by Bernard Picart (1673–1733) such as his 'Diverses modes dessinées d'après nature', which includes a charming informal lady in summer dress, provide the only alternative in this context to the hierarchic and formal images of Les Modes.

The Régence, 1715 to 1750, ushered in a period of greater informality reflected by a change of feminine fashion. This change can be seen in the paintings by Antoine Watteau (1684–1721), but not too clearly in the sets of engravings from his work, *Figures Françoises et Comiques Nouvellement Inventées par M. Watteau*, and *Figures de Modes Dessinées et Gravées à l'eau forte, par Watteau et terminées au burin par Thomassin le fils* (n.d.). In these, theatrical and conventional dress are mingled without explanatory captions. Not until the mid to late 1720s did illustrations concerned only with fashionable dress begin to appear. This was a development to be observed coincidentally on either side of the Channel.

In England, Bernard Lens (1682–1740), the enameller and miniature painter, made two large but overlapping sets of bust and half-length pen and wash pictures of ladies, but included a few gentlemen. This series was entitled 'The exact dress of the head drawn from life at the court, the opera, etc', and the main interest lies in the minute differences in arrangement of the ladies' caps and lappets and the gentlemen's wigs and hats. So far no reason has been discovered why these drawings were made since they were never published. One set is in the Royal Collection at Windsor, and another in the Victoria and Albert Museum.

In France, *Figures Françoises Nouvellement Inventées par Octavien . . .* (1725) show front and back views of a lady in the new low headdress and flowing unfitted *robe volante*, and a gentleman in loosely-fitting coat and fringed waistcoat with the softly-curling wig that was fashionable at that time. These are slight but clear little images of fashions which were to be shown more explicitly by Antoine Hérisset (1685–1769), better known for his engravings of Versailles, in his *Recueil des Differentes Modes du Temps* dated 1729; these consist of eleven plates, five of men's clothes and six of ladies', each having two or three views to show all sides, with the names of the garments engraved on each plate. The title-page is an arrangement of accessories, and the fact that the set was obtainable from the engraver, '*chez un frippier*' (a clothes dealer), may be significant. The clothes are remarkably up to date. 'Redingotes' (riding or over-coats) are described as a fashion new from England, in the 'Mercure de France' of 1728, and a manuscript reference to fashions for 1729 mentions '*vestes et parements d'etoffe d'or*' (waistcoats and coats trimmed with cloth of gold). For women there are '*Les Manteaux*' (gowns with draped trains), *Les Bagnolettes* (hoods), *Les Mantilles* (capes), *Les Casaquins* (hip length gowns) and *Les Mantes* (mantles), while for men there are also *Les habits ordinaires* (everyday suits), *Les Manches en pagode* (coats with wide flaring cuffs) and *Les Perrukes à faces* (wigs with queues).

The shortage of fashion plates at this period is less tantalizing than for previous centuries, because from this date there is an increasing quantity of actual surviving garments and an abundance of portraits and genre scenes. Few of these have the sense of style and movement of Hubert Gravelot's three sets of fashionable figures made in 1745 during his stay in England, engraved by Truchy, Grignion and Major and published by Bowles. They have no titles but some are marked as having been drawn from life, and they are as elegant as they are realistic. The men, seated and standing, wear conventional clothes not too precisely differentiated; the twelve women show a variety of views of the main types of English fashionable gown: the informal open robe and petticoat, the sack, a robe with pleats flowing from the back of the shoulders, a development of the *robe volante*, and the mantua, similar to that shown in Hérisset, though more formal.

By the second half of the 18th century it is evident that there was a demand both for the commercial and the primarily artistic engraved fashion plate. The former, somewhat stunted and summary likenesses of the latest fashions, found their way with increasing regularity into publications like the almanacs. Among English periodicals, the *Lady's Magazine* of 1759 is credited with showing the first. They were intended for a fast-increasing feminine readership and these small plates, rather crudely engraved 'dresses of the year', must have done much to bring provincial fashions in line with those of the metropolis. Many of these plates are not in their original publications but were cut out and stuck in scrapbooks.

English fashion plates were also exported. During his visit to England, in 1774–5, Lichtenburg, the Göttingen Professor of Physics, sent them regularly to his friend the German publisher Dieterich. As the almanacs were normally not available until November for the following year, Dieterich was always worried in case they would be out of date by the time he could publish them in Germany.

Such copying soon lapsed because the plates in English almanacs do not bear comparison with the fine and lively engravings of Daniel Chodowiecki (1726–1801), [*] the Danzig-born painter working in Berlin, who was making them for the German almanacs and periodicals between the late 1770s and the late 1780s. They are small in size but have a quality hitherto lacking and never common in fashion plates, a graceful and totally endearing sense of the ridiculous. Ernst Ludwig Riepenhuisen (1765–1840) continued to make similar small fashion plates until the end of the century.

By the last decade of the century, the German publishing houses were in a prime position to take over from the French as the Ancien Régime disintegrated under political pressures. There were many magazines, the most important being, in Weimar, the long running *Journal der Luxus und der Moden* (1786–1826,) and, in Leipzig, the *Journal für Fabrik, Manufaktur und Handlung und Mode* (1791–1808). Innovatory as they were in many ways, not least in the systematic coverage of German, French and English fashion, they lacked artistic distinction and their plates, sometimes rather crude in colour, were only too easily recognised as copies of more refined originals.

French engraving reached the height of its achievement during the last half of the 18th century. There was a large and growing clientele, especially among the middle classes, increasingly receptive to new tastes and ideas. Fashion flourished in a society obsessed with personal extravagance. It was at this market that the enterprising publishers Jean Esnaut and Michel Rapilly aimed the first extended sets of fashion plates, a development of the 17th and early 18th century 'Modes' series, but in more sophisticated form. These sets of prints were to become the 'Galeries des Modes'. Basset, engraver and *marchand mercier*, made a formal complaint in 1777 that they had copied his idea of a 'Manuel des Toillettes' – a set of head-dresses – causing him loss and, in their embellishments of his idea, causing discredit both to him and the French nation. His complaint sheds new light on publishing attitudes at the time. Basset finds the title 'Galerie' pompous and of doubtful copyright and their innovation, figures in conversation piece settings, not '*animés . . . gracieux interessants*' but '*lascives*'. He takes particular exception to the lady in her peignoir washing her feet, another tying her garter in the presence of her male companion and the tailor adjusting a ladies corset, describing them as '*Toutes figures obscenes qui choquent l'oeil honnête, et n'amuse que les libertins*'. He is even more horrified that they have a portrait collection which will include the Royal Family.

Between 1776 and 1787, Esnaut and Rapilly were to publish, in colour and black and white, 78 sets of head dresses and 342 sets of fashions, mainly for women but also for men and children. The day clothes were comparatively simple, the formal ones increasingly elaborate.

It is possible to observe how the artist arranged the same trimmings in different combinations to satisfy the demand for quantity rather than quality of design. Possibly the best way to see them is to consult the annotated facsimile edition by Paul Cornu. The freedom of line and inventiveness of Le Clère, Desrais, Watteau de Lisle and Gabriel de Saint Aubin lose little in reproduction, though the colour does become a little flat.

The plates were also exported, and the *Lady's Magazine* in England slipped into the habit of re-engraving and reproducing the occasional style, under the heading *New Paris fashions*. The text, except in the first two cumulative volumes, was minimal, but this gap was filled by the *Cabinet des Modes*, launched by the young Le Brun Tossa in 1785. It continued under various titles until 1792 and provided frequent, regular and up-to-date coverage of all fashionable novelties from clothes to carriages. It is very useful for its illustrations of accessories. It was aimed at an international market, a feature stressed when the title was changed in 1786 to *Magasin des Modes nouvelles françaises et anglaises*, but it seems without much success for copies are rare in England. Detached plates are not uncommon and many of the illustrations can be found copied in the German fashion periodicals.

Le Brun Tossa was concerned for the quality of his prints, especially good in the middle period, and from an editorial we learn that each of the plates, unfortunately unsigned, took a day to draw, that the etching was finished in dry point and that they were coloured in gouache not water colour, taking twice as long to produce as similar works and costing proportionately more.

The *Monument du Costume* illustrates French concern with fashion at its most elevated, even philosophical, level. The three sets which form the *Suite d'estampes pour servir a l'histoire des moeurs et du costume des Français dans le dix-huitième siècle'*, 1775, 1777 and 1783, published by Prault at the instigation of Eberts, the banker and connoisseur, consciously promote refined French taste, styles and way of life as the model for the world. Their faith in the artists Moreau le Jeune and Freudenburg, responsible for the greater part of the plates, was justified. They have made these well-dressed and impeccably-furnished genre scenes as acceptable to posterity as they were to their contemporaries, exemplars of the truly tasteful rather than the merely modish. The sets are linked by a rather garrulous text written by that very practical amorist and litterateur, Restif de la Bretonne. He is hardly at his best providing material for *L'histoire morale*.

The first part is concerned with the life of *une femme de bon ton*, from her entry into society to the birth of her first child; the second celebrates the delights of maternity (both of these rather Rousseauesque in their sentiment); the third covers the daily pursuits of a well-connected young man.

In spite of its elevated tone, the work had a practical aim. After all, Eberts was a banker. In the first and second prefaces, the editors stress the use of the engravings as models for artists, theatrical and fashion designers and as a pattern book for good French artifacts. It was a pious hope, for the sets were expensive and slow to appear. Their greatest use is to posterity as a record of the fine French craftsmanship during the reign of Louis XVI. It was an idealisation of a way of life on the brink of dissolution, the swan song of the Ancien Régime.

At first it seemed that the social upheaval of the Revolution would destroy French leadership of fashion. One bibliographer can find no trace of any French fashion journals at all from 1794–7. Enterprise was not killed, but it was dispersed, greatly to England's benefit. Niklaus von Heideloff, a member of a long established Leipzig family of court artists, who had been working as a miniature painter, emigrated from Paris during the troubles and found refuge in London. He started his *Gallery of Fashion* in 1794, the year in which even the determined Le Brun Tossa ceased production. There is a conscious nationalism in the preface to his fine series of fashion aquatints, which were to continue until 1804. Heideloff promised his subscribers a 'collection of the most fashionable and elegant Dresses in Vogue ... the first and only one published in this country; it surpasses anything of the kind formerly published at Paris', and indeed it did. It was expensive, costing initially three guineas a year for approximately thirty plates in twelve numbers, and it was published by subscription. The dresses, he wrote, were copied by permission from 'those worn by ladies of rank and fashion' to whom, if they wished (apparently they did not) he would give the credit. The dressmakers were less shy.

The fashions are not at all French and are exceedingly modest and voluminous. The ladies who wear them are dignified and pretty, if rather robust. The backgrounds, more frequent in the middle period, are economical and attractive. There are no risqué captions and no men. Heideloff obviously agreed with M. Basset on the necessity for propriety. Heideloff's aim of 'interesting ladies of the highest fashion ... and admirers of the fine arts by providing images of the highest quality' succeeded. His subscription list indicates a steady rise in numbers and social tone. By 1797, his readers included Queen Charlotte, the Empress of Germany, members of the German and English aristocracy, the Russian and Turkish ambassadors and the art dealers Colnaghi and Ackermann.

Despite the war with France, other journals were less nationalistic than the patriotic Mr Heideloff. All of them included fashion news from France, though the poor quality of the engraving, especially in that long-time friend of English womanhood, *The Lady's Magazine*, as well as the extreme ultra-classical styles of the Directoire, make it difficult to decide whether they were designed to allure or patriotically deter a British readership. It is also significant that even at a time of war Robert Phillips could start a new journal, *The Magazine of the Female Fashions of London and Paris*. It lasted from 1798 to 1806 and usually one third of the fashions shown were French.

The play on words, *La Belle Assemblée*, the title chosen by the English publisher John Bell for his new ladies' magazine in 1806, confirms the *'franglais'* character of fashion publishing at that time. In his organisation of the contents with a separate clear and systematic advertising supplement he was a pioneer, just as he was with his typography. The plates have what may be called a consistent inconsistency. The earliest are black and white but by the next year, possibly influenced by the short-lived *Le Beau Monde* (1806–8) which was edited by his son and competitor J. R. Bell and which included good colour plates of both men's and women's fashions, he was using colour. Skilled English water-colourists and engravers contributed; the names Devis, James Mitan, John and William Hopwood all appear, though not necessarily on the best plates which are irritatingly anonymous. The magazine continued until 1836, though as John Bell got older there was a fall in quality.

Rudolph Ackermann's *Repository of Arts Literature Commerce Manufactures Fashion and Politics* (1809–28) was another journal which profited from the dispersal of talent which resulted from the French Revolution. Ackermann was born in Stuttgart, where he had trained as an engraver, and had gone to Paris where he became a designer of carriages. He came to England and by 1796 had founded a water colour school with a print and fancy goods shop which by 1809 was the largest in London, employing fifty people. He was known for his charity, especially to refugees, many of whom he employed, and he could hardly have regretted his patronage of Niklaus von Heideloff. The *Repository*, edited by F. Schoberl, was a general in-terest magazine of a kind new to England and intended to appeal to both men and women. The illustrations, many of which are aquatints, are of the highest quality. The fashion plates have great and consistent charm with the figures sometimes gracefully posed with an article of furniture, also of the latest design. They are all anonymous, either through artists's preference or editorial policy, though Ackermann usually acknowl-edged the work of the artists and engravers of his non-periodical works like the *Microcosms*.

From the biography of Thomas Uwins (1782–1827), who designed many of the plates from 1809, we learn that to Ackermann they were merely 'preddy faces' and worth half a crown apiece. It is interesting to speculate on whether Ackermann was influenced by the enlightened design policy of the *Cabinet des Modes*. His debt to the German publications is much easier to trace. One of the most popular features of the magazine was the heraldic plate of *Patterns of British Manufacture* to which were affixed small squares of fashionable textiles. This was not his invention but first appeared in 1791 in the *Journal für Fabrik Manufaktur und Hand-lung und Mode*, a publication of which he must surely have known.

As the long war with its blockade continued, English fashion and fashion plates slowly settled into an agree-able English style. It was a surprise and not altogether a pleasant one for English visitors to Paris during the First Peace of Paris in 1814 to see the fashion changes that had taken place. Horace Vernet's views of them in the *Bon Genre* are valid if satirical comment on the effect of isolation on national taste.

While the ladies did not seem to be indifferent to the changes in fashion which had taken place in France during the war, the publishers paid little attention to the important new developments in the style and format of French fashion plates. These developments owed much to the publisher Pierre La Mésangère, former priest and professor of philosophy who took over the two-year-old *Journal des Dames et des Modes* in 1799. It had been the first fashion journal to start after the break in 1794–7. His influence was such that rather confusingly the journal was known simply as *La Mésangère*. His contribution is most clearly seen in the sets of separate but related plates on fashionable themes.

As engraved by Debucourt the fifty-two plates of *Modes et Manières du Jour* ... (1801–10) bring a new elegance and ease to the genre. Unfortunately complete sets are very scarce.

La Mésangère commissioned from the young Horace Vernet, Debucourt's friend, the thirty-four-plate set *Incroyables et Merveilleuses* (1814). According to the newly-wed Madame Vernet's account book he paid eighty francs apiece. Engraved by Gatine and Lanté, they are vigorous and extrovert, and specific in their fashion detail. Their subjects make an interesting contrast with the Incroyables and Merveilleuses that his father Carle Vernet had drawn during the Directoire. Horace Vernet continued to design fashion plates for La Mésangère regularly between 1811 and 1816, for which he was paid fifty francs each. When his income rose after the sale of his first large painting, he appears to have abandoned his fashion plate commissions.

The sheer prettiness of the clothes of the 1830s may make us indifferent to the stereotyped poses and arrangement of the fashion plates, but it was a problem which concerned Henri de Girardon who, with Honoré de Balzac, founded a new society journal, La Mode, in 1829. In his introductory editorial he deplores the 'well-dressed doll' of conventional contemporary fashion illustration. He found someone to revitalise it in Gavarni, who had recommended himself by the charm as well as the humanity of his series of Travestissements or fancy dresses. It is a pity that La Mode or the other journals to which he contributed are so rare in England, for the lively little figures are both human and fashionable. Despite his popularity, high fees and social success – he was said to be one of the best looking men of his time – Gavarni became increasingly bored with fashion work and as soon as he could turned to the darker realism of his lithographs. His little Grisettes are as pretty as his fashion models but much more enduring and worldly-wise.

By the middle of the 19th century French domination of the luxury trades was again complete. The links between the journals and the couturiers became closer, though as yet little is known of the details of the arrangements made. French fashions were an important export and the most popular of the magazines became what we would now call international co-editions, changing text but not plates according to the country in which they appeared. Die Modenwelt, known as The Season, is said to have appeared in fourteen different languages. Le Follet is perhaps the best known in England. A reason for their domination of the market was the generally high quality of their fashion plates. They are usually signed or marked with the name of the artist and engraver and sometimes have a publisher's imprint. Frederick Goubaud was one of the most important. He provided fancy work patterns as well as fashion plates and his imprint is to be found in several of the journals. We know something about the arrangements that he made when the Englishwoman's Domestic Magazine decided in 1860 to issue hand-coloured plates

engraved after Jules David, one of the best designers of these plates, who also worked for Le Journal des Modes.

Fashion plates became small conversation pieces with illustrations of ladies, and sometimes children but rarely men, doing not very much against a fitting, sometimes fussy but never over-assertive background. None lack charm but they do sometimes become rather stereotyped and sloppy: small wonder, considering the sheer quantity that had to be produced. In a few instances the original water colours exist, much fresher and more vigorous than the engraved and sometimes rather worn plates which appeared in the magazines.

The Colin family dominated what had now become an industry, between the 1840s and the 1870s. They are a link between the inventiveness of La Mésangère and the grace and skill of the English draughtsmen and watercolourists. Alexander Colin (1798–1875) has been described as an artist of mediocre quality, but he was a pupil of Girodet and Les Deveria and a friend of Delacroix and Bonington. Both he and his wife drew fashion plates and the lives of all his children show the continued close connection between the Paris art world and that of fashion illustration. His son Paul Alfred became a landscape painter, but his three daughters were between them responsible for the greater part of the plates produced in Paris during the middle of the 19th century: Heloise (1820–74) married the painter Auguste Leloir, Anais (1822–99) married the architect Gabriele Toudouze, and the third daughter Laure (1827–92) married the painter Gregoire Noël. Anais's daughter Isobel carried the tradition on into the next generation, and between them the family illustrated every change of style from crinoline to bustle. Through Maurice Leloir, the costume designer, fashion historian and founder member of the French Costume Society as well as historical adviser to Douglas Fairbanks in Hollywood, the family still continue to influence the popular image of past fashions. Of course the names of other designers also appeared on fashion plates, but for the most part they were active in other forms of book illustration as well.

English dependence on France was so complete that when communication with Paris was shut off during the siege of 1870, Le Follet was stricken with panic. The editor wrote of the necessity for bravery during the crisis, apologetically proffered Belgian plates and uncoloured English ones and in a subsequent issue published several pages of press congratulations upon his bravery in so doing.

Paris fashion survived the fall of the Third Empire and Haute Couture became an increasingly important part of an expanding French fashion industry. Initially the couturiers seemed unwilling to lose their exclusive-ness by publicising their models, so most of the names under the plates are those of the Confection, the ready-to-wear and exportation branch of the trade, but during the last quarter of the century this slowly began to change.

Many but not all the illustrations of the time do little more than show the clothes on elongated doe-eyed stereotypes. Perhaps the reason is partly economic, because there was tremendous competition from a large number of cheaper publications during this period aimed at an enormously expanded middle class readership and a newly literate lower class market. Pricing was keen, as demonstrated by the calculations Isabella Beeton made in her diary to justify the purchase of plates and patterns from M. Goubaud. However, prices were lower than they had been before the re-moval of English tariffs on French luxury goods in 1860. Traditional methods of magazine production were also beginning to change with the introduction of new printing methods and different quality of paper.

Another reason for the degeneration of the fashion plate may well have been the influence of the photo-graph. By the last quarter of the century realism in representation had become unfashionable. The camera had been used by draughtsmen and engravers since its introduction in the 1840s, and photography was now beginning to creep into fashion illustration, especially in men's tailoring plates. It was not in direct competition with the fashion drawing because photographic repro-duction in printed journals, though technically feasible, was not common until the end of the century. There were also aesthetic problems: without retouching, which was somewhat expensive, the camera made the ladies look fat.

It was Charles Adolphe Sandoz who, working in Paris, revived the fashion plate in its traditional con-versation piece form. The work of this Ukrainian-born architect-trained painter and illustrator is seen in full flower in the couture plates in *The Queen* during the 1890s. The scale of his achievement can be seen by studying his early work during the late 1870s and 1880s in *La Revue de Mode*. The atmosphere is reminiscent of the *Monument du Costume*, a resemblance heightened by conscious echoes of Louis Seize in the high style décor of the Nineties which Osbert Lancaster has so aptly called *Le Style Rothschild*. It seems probable that he drew the clothes from the photographic records of the Couture houses—by this time an accepted use of photography in fashion. The *placement* and graceful pose of the figures are his own and a little reminiscent of Tissot.

Black and white work became increasingly popular at the turn of the century. It was a fashionable trend in the art world and in this context it had the advantage of being easier and cheaper to reproduce in the many new magazines as well as the newspapers which had a regular ladies' section. One of the most popular illustrators, Georges Pilotelle, is credited with the invention of the 'seven foot beauty with the ten inch waist'. His work is slightly *art nouveau* in character and his busy sinuous line is well suited to the slender 'S' bend figure and soft trimmings of the period. Another popular fashion plate artist was 'Mr Albert Collins . . . known as the Sargent of Fashion Plate delineators'. Bessie Ayscough's work in the *Morning Chronicle* was an inspiration to the young Cecil Beaton. The drawings of Charles Dana Gibson, originator of the Gibson girl, though not fashion plates, certainly influenced both contemporary fashions and fashion plate artists.

The revolutionary change in fashion ushered in by Paul Poiret in his early collections with simple lines and vivid 'sunbursts of colour' required a new technique to do them justice. Poiret was in any case unlikely to be content with the outworn conventions of the 19th century artists. His mentor was Jacques Doucet, couturier and discriminating art collector, who had replaced his 18th-century masterpieces with Picasso and Les Fauves. Dunoyer de Segonzac designed Poiret's first letter-heads, and in Paul Iribe and Georges Lepape he found artists capable of responding to the essential qualities of his clothes. Iribe's *Les Robes de Paul Poiret* of 1908 and Georges Lepape's *Les Choses de Paul Poiret* (1911) return to the simplicity of the early 19th-century format. They have a Japanese clarity of shape and the stencil process gives oriental brilliance to the colours. The books were limited editions printed on hand-made paper with-out any text. They were advertisements of such enig-matic refinement that Queen Alexandra showed in-credible perspicacity but not taste when she had the Iribe returned as a trade catalogue.

It was the *Gazette du Bon Ton* founded by the pub-lisher Lucien Vogel in 1912 which brought work of this quality to a wider public. He came by chance upon the sketches of a group of young artists, friends and fellow students: Bernard Boutet de Monvel, Jacques and Pierre Brissaud who, with Georges Barbier, Jean Besnard, A. E. Marty, Charles Martin, Paul Iribe and Georges Lepape became the founding contributors of the magazine.

Simple anecdotal settings, reminiscent of the La Mésangère series, brilliantly stencil coloured, are used to show the clothes of the couture sponsors of the work – Cheruit, Doeillet, Doucet, Lanvin, Poiret, Redfern and

Worth. This pattern was followed in other journals: *Journal des Dames et des Modes*, *Modes et Manières d'Aujourd'hui*, *Les Feuillets d'Art* and *Art Goût et Beauté*. Their plates are now collector's pieces.

Magazines of this quality were expensive and the work of these artists and those associated with them, Erté, Benito and Bruneleschi, did not reach a wider public until *Bon Ton* and other Vogel interests were bought by Condé-Nast for *Vogue* in the late 1920s. For the next few years their charming illustrations in black and white only continued the *art deco* tradition, and they were to be found in *Vogue* and its rival, *Harper's Bazaar*. Erté had an exclusive contract for the cover of *Harper's Bazaar* until 1932 when the determined new editor, Carmel Snow, tried to oust him. This was a sign of the times and marked the return to a livelier, less formal attitude to illustration. Ernest Dryden, the German illustrator associated with *Die Dame* was an artist whose work spans both styles.

The competition between these two magazines for artists and now also for photographers of quality has been told in a number of memoirs. The editors and art directors of both *Harper's Bazaar* and *Vogue* should share the credit for the revival of fashion illustration in the 1930s. Besides Carmel Snow, Lucian Vogel was still active and there were also Dr Agha and Michael de Brunhoff of *Vogue*.

There was now a new tradition in black and white work, fluid and semi-realistic. This can be seen in the works of the English Cecil Beaton and Francis Marshall. As the economic situation began to improve in the mid 1930s, colour plates returned. Carl Erickson, the Swedish-American artist, recorded the social scene with honesty and elegance and was rivalled only by René Bouet Willaumez, his Breton-born colleague on *Vogue*. Perhaps the most attractive and evocative plates were by Christian 'Bébé' Bérard, romantic painter and stage designer, a discovery of the artistically adventurous Carmel Snow. She used both Jean Cocteau and Marcel Vertés to illustrate clothes, and was never afraid of the non-explicit as long as it was effective. Bérard was not popular with Randolph Hearst, the proprietor of *Harper's Bazaar*, who called him 'Faceless Freddy' from his habit of ignoring the features of his subjects, but it was the *Vogue* editors who left the more detailed memoirs of the traumas of working with him. He was obsessed with fashion but bored with making fashion drawings. Nevertheless his high speed impressionist gouaches ('stains on the paper become birds and flowers') convey all the excitement and colour of the designer's intentions.

The era of the fashion artist came to an end in 1939, for the post-war years have belonged to the artist-photographer, not the illustrator.

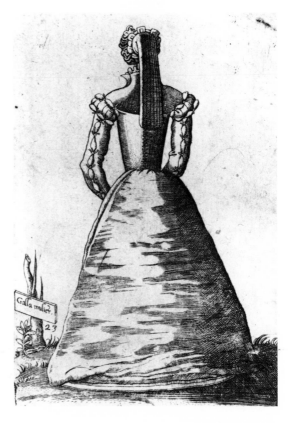

PLATES I, 2

A Lady of France, front and back view engraved by Enea Vico (1523–67) for *Habitus Nostrae Aetatis*, 1556. The earliest set of costume engravings of this kind and much copied. Ferdinando Bertelli includes these and many other plates by Vico, usually in reverse, in his *Omnium Fere' Gentium Nostrae Aetatis Habitus, Nunquam Ante Hac Aediti*, 1563 and 1569

The lady wears the stiff-boned bodice and cone-shaped skirt conventional for the third quarter of the 16th century in both France and England, but not easy to see in portraits of the time as a gown often concealed the shape. The very low neckline, only partially shaded by a transparent vest (which contemporary English ladies would have called a 'partlet'), recalls some of the descriptions of the appearance and dress of Queen Elizabeth I. Perhaps this lady also was unmarried. There is no text apart from the caption, so comment is conjectural. The back view shows the laced fastening of the bodice and, just above the hemline, the farthingale or stiffened petticoat. The pendant lappet at the back of the cap is the last trace of the mediaeval hood, from which it developed.
E.702/3–1903.

Nobilis Anglus.   Nobilis matrona in Anglia.   Virgo in Anglia.   Nobilis fæmina in Anglia.   Nobilis Anglus.

Fæmina Londinensis ornatus.   Ciuis Londinensis honesta vestitu.   Nobilis matrona in Anglia.   Nobilis in Anglia.   Iuuenis Anglus.

3

4   Cortigiana Veneta

5   Cortigiana Veneta

6

PLATE 3

Some people of England, engraving by Abraham de Bruyn (1540–1587), *Omnium Poene Europae, Asiae, Aphricae Atque Americae Gentium Habitus . . . Michel Colÿn Excudit,* 1581.

A popular and much plagiarized work. Styles have changed in the quarter century since PLATES 1, 2; the ladies begin to dress their hair higher at the temples; skirts and sleeves are fuller; the collar frill has become the ruff. Gowns are worn by both men and women and the breeches now have 'canions' reaching to the knee. Note that the 'Civis Londoniensis Honesta Vestitu' is described as wearing ordinary dress, the distinctive and somewhat archaic characteristics of which – flat cap and long-skirted doublet – may suggest class and status.

E.1656–1899

PLATES 4, 5

A Venetian Courtesan, engraving by Pietro Bertelli (1580–1616) from his *Diversarum Nationum Habitus . . .* Padua, 1593 (1st edition 1589).

The aim of the Trachtenbuch was to illustrate the diversity of dress, national, regional or occupational. Venetian costume always aroused comment and visitors were fascinated by the distinctive clothes worn by courtesans and prostitutes. The coiffure with the horn-like curls, frequently sun-bleached, and the high 'chopines' (clogs), an obvious convenience in this often-flooded city, are typically Venetian. However, the masculine-style breeches were peculiar to the profession and to be seen only by the reader with sufficient experience to know what might lie beneath the skirt.

Library

PLATE 6

A Noblewoman, drawn and engraved by Jacques Callot (1592–1635) for his *La Noblesse de Lorraine,* 1624.

Her wide full hair style, deep overlapping collars, puffed sleeves and high waistline are all conventional at this date. The overskirt, looped up for convenience and decorative effect, shows the contrasting petticoat beneath.

E.986–1961

PLATE 7

A nobleman, engraved by Abraham Bosse (1602–1676) after Jean de Saint-Igny (? d. 1647) from *Le Jardin de la Noblesse Fran çoise dans Lequel ce Peut Ceuillir Leur Manierre de Vettements,* 1629.

His doublet is shorter-waisted and has deeper skirts, while the breeches are longer and looser than in the 16th century, and are altogether easier and more comfortable. The slashing of the sleeve gives extra ease of movement. New are the wide-brimmed plumed hat, flowing hair, lace-trimmed flat collar and loose-fitting riding boots, features popularly if not entirely accurately associated with 'Cavaliers', the English Civil War and Dumas' *Three Musketeers.* It is possible that he is slightly old-fashioned, because a new-style simple curving sleeve is worn by another nobleman from this series. The ribbon 'points', internal ties holding doublet to breeches which are clearly visible at the hips, were soon to be replaced with more convenient metal hooks and eyes.

26334–4

7

15

Nobilis Mulier Aulica Anglicana.

9

8

10

PLATES 8, 9, 10

English ladies, drawn and engraved by Wenceslaus Hollar (1607–1677). PLATE 8 from *Ornatus Muliebris Anglicanus or the Severall Habits of Englishwomen*, 1640. PLATES 9, 10 from the *Theatrum Mulierum*, 1643.

The clothes illustrate the change in style from the 1630s to the 1640s. The dresses before 1640 are much more high-waisted and have fuller sleeves and skirt. Those after 1640 have the deep pointed waistline which was to remain fashionable for almost a quarter of a century. The back view (10) shows the hood normally worn outdoors, and the draping of the skirt to keep the train from trailing in the mud. Hollar's talent in depicting texture is shown in the fur muff and tie carried by the lady in PLATE 8 and in the pinked or tufted fabric of her dress.

1944–98   20767–35   20767–53

PLATES 11, 12

A lady and gentleman, *circa* 1670 from *Figures à la Mode Inventez et Gravez par R. de Hooge et Mis en Lumiere par N. Visscher*. Romain de Hoog(h)e (1665–1708), a Dutch engraver, may have been working in Paris when he drew these flamboyantly fashionable figures.

The gentleman wears the new 'justeaucorps', a knee-length loose coat, and a waistcoat over his beribboned breeches. The cut can be more easily seen on the simpler version worn by his servant. Ribbon trimming became fashionable when French sumptuary legislation forbade the use of metal braid and embroidery. The lady's gown is very broad at the shoulder and long in the waist. The mid-point of change between this fashion and the Hollar (PLATE 9) can be seen in the dress of the maid, which is plainer and in older style. It is possible that the loops at the waist were used to pull up a trailing skirt. The lady wears a veil-cum-hood protecting both her complexion and her discretion.

E.1445/8–1897

13

14

15

16

Ladies and gentlemen of 1688 and 1693, engraved by
Jean de St Jean (before 1671–after 1709). PLATES 13, 14,
dated 1688, the woman 'en Sultane'. PLATES 15, 16 dated
1693, the woman 'en Stenkerke et falbala'.

Typical of the engravings of fashions and the fashionable
that were produced in Paris during the late 17th and early
18th century. The ladies wear an overgown, the 'manteau'
(in England the 'mantua'), a development of the loose
robe of Eastern origin introduced for informal wear in
the third quarter of the 17th century. It is pleated to shape
over the corset, which had replaced the boned 'stiff-
bodied' gown formerly in fashion (see PLATE 12). The
term 'Sultane' may suggest its oriental place of origin or
refer more specifically to the fastenings attached to the
front border. The sleeves are short, and the ruffles of the
chemise appear below the turn-back cuffs. In PLATE 15
the train is looped back to show the petticoat; 'falbala'
refers to the frilled trimming. In the five years between
PLATES 13 and 15 the gown had become tighter and the·
waist and sleeves longer, an elongation of line confirmed
by the taller narrower coiffure. Hair began to be dressed
high off the forehead about 1680, a style associated with
Mlle de Fontanges, mistress of Louis XIV, and popularly
if not too accurately named after her.

The gentlemen (PLATES 14, 16) wear coats and waistcoats,
tighter and more shapely versions of the justeaucorps
(PLATE 11). Here too there is formalization and an elongation of line, with the later coat tighter and having longer
sleeves and lower-set pockets. Trimming is restrained,
though colours were often bright and ribbons, like those
at the cravat (PLATE 16), were out of fashion by the end of
the century. The 'Stenkerke', or steenkirke, is a twisted
neckcloth so called after the battle fought there in 1692,
when the French officers were said to have been hurried
to knot their cravats. In the main it was a masculine style.
Hat brims were turned up in the more precise three-
corner shape that was to remain fashionable for almost
the next hundred years. Long curling wigs were still in
fashion, having been so since about 1660.

(13) E.26363 4
(14) E.26363 18
(15) E.26363 3
(16) E.26363 15

PLATE 17
A Lady, drawn and engraved from life, by François
Octavien (1695–1732) from his *Figures Françoises Nouvelle-
ment Inventées . . .* Paris, 1725.

She wears another development of the loose robe with
pleats falling straight from shoulder to hem. It was an
informal dress: in France it would have been called a
'Robe Volante', but in England, where at this time it
was not very popular nor considered quite respectable in
its resemblance to the 18th century version of the dressing
gown, 'a sack'. It is a relaxed style and predictable perhaps
in the less formal atmosphere of the French Régence,
1715–51. It is often shown in the paintings and engravings
of Watteau, and in consequence is sometimes retrospec-
tively called 'Plis Watteau'.
E.3249–1922

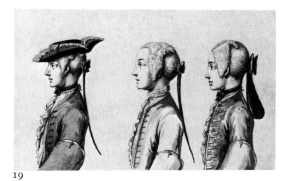

18

19

PLATES 18, 19

Head-dresses for men and women from a series of pen and ink wash drawings by Bernard Lens (1682–1740) from his *The Exact Dress of the Head Drawn from Life at the Court and Opera . . . 1725–26.*

There are 87 in the series, and most of the ladies wear their hair dressed close to the head, with a slight wave at the forehead, and the remainder swept smoothly to a knot concealed invariably by a cap. Unusual is the lady who has her hair curled in a style imported from France. As for the caps, the series shows more than six dozen in muslin and lace variations on the limited theme of front frill, crown and lappet. The very slight front emphasis is all that remains of the towering head-dresses of late 17th and early 18th century, quite suddenly unfashionable after 1712–13.

The first gentleman wears a three-cornered hat and the others show off the wig, with the hair flat curled in front. The 'pig tail', or 'queue', was covered in black silk to protect the coat from being marked by the powder with which the wig was dressed. The 'pig tail' was more informal than the 'bag' wig. By this period, the long full-bottomed wig was becoming old-fashioned and sometimes a sign of professional dignity.

E.1677, 1681–1926

PLATE 20, 21

French Fashions for 1729, drawn and engraved by Antoine Hérisset (1685–1769) for his *Recueil des Differentes Modes du Temps à Paris . . . 1729.*

The ladies wear 'Les Manteaux', a form of gown now distinguished only by having the back of the skirt pleated and draped. Reactionary in styling, it is a formal dress for which the new-fashioned and probably expensive silk woven in 'lace pattern', shown to advantage on the wide skirt, would have been eminently suitable, Skirts of this size would have needed the support of hooped petticoats, introduced in England in 1714 and in France by 1719. The sleeves are wide, the fullness controlled by vertical pleating, and the headdress is low and covered by the dark silk hood commonly worn outdoors.

The men wear 'Les Redingotes' which were so called by the French because they were of English origin and preferred for riding and travelling as less cumbersome than the cloak. They are distinguished by a form of storm collar, and it is probable that the pockets are in the side seams. A description of them in articles on tailoring in *Encyclopédie ou Dictionnaire des Sciences*, Paris 1765–70, suggests they changed but little in 20 years. The central figure also shows the fashionable coat and waistcoat. Pockets are set at waist level and the skirts are widely flared. Coat cuffs, to be seen on other plates in the series, are similar to those of the 'Redingote': heavy and deep, reaching from wrist to elbow.

E.3255/62–1913

20

21

22

23

PLATES 22, 23

An English lady and gentleman, dated 1744–5, drawn by Hubert François Gravelot (1699–1773). PLATE 22 engraved by L. Truchy and PLATE 23 engraved by T. Major.

The lady 'drawn *Ad Vivum*' wears typical English informal everyday dress, a loose open-fronted gown with a neckerchief covering the decolletage corset and stomacher and an apron over the petticoat. The back of the bodice would have been shaped by stitched pleats. Possibly she wears side hoops, but a quilted petticoat was a popular and effective substitute. The sleeves are shorter and wider than in 1729 but the cuffs similar, allowing the shift ruffles to show. Her cap is covered by her wide flat hat drawn tight to the head with ribbons.

The gentleman, PLATE 23, wears a coat closer and longer-fitting in the body than in PLATE 21 though the skirts remain wide. Pockets are at hip level where they will remain until the end of the century. Sleeves have become longer with cuffs slightly less deep than those of 1730. The hair tied back in a 'queue' could have been his own or a wig. Cravats, unusual in informal dress such as this, are replaced by the frill on the shirt.

(22)   E.2239A–1886
(23)   E.1070–1886

PLATE 24

A Lady in the Dress of the Year 1759, anonymous engraving for a Lady's almanac or pocketbook, wears a 'sack' as her semi-formal dress. This gown is now an accepted part of the English wardrobe and a tighter and more formal arrangement of the pleats shows off the neat corsetted figure to advantage. The slim trim line, typical of the later 1750s and 1760s, is thrown into relief by the frills, usually in a matching colour, at cuffs, on the sleeves and at the openings of the robe and on the petticoat. Decoratively they have a chiaroscuro rococo effect and replace the former taste for colour contrasts and embroidery.

E.488–1902

PLATES 25, 26

Fashionable Styles from Germany, drawn and engraved for almanacs by Daniel Nicolaus Chodowiecki (1726–1801).

PLATE 25: The gentlemen of Berlin in 1780 wear 1. riding dress, with double-breasted coat, and boots; 2. 'Full dress' rather on the French style; 3/4. everyday dress, the older man with more formal and rather older fashioned cocked hat and tightly cut coat, while the younger man wears up to date loose fitting countryfied styling and the new fashioned small round hat, said to be based on the riding hat. Engraved for the Genealogischer Kalender auf das Jahr, 1780, Lauenburg.

PLATE 26: The ladies of Berlin in 1779 are dressed in the French style and the figures show 1. Court dress; 2. Semi-formal dress; 3/4. Gowns caught up for ease of movement. Engraved for the Genealogischer Kalender auf das Jahr, 1779, Lauenburg.

(25)   29447–1
(26)   201566–3

25

24

26

Bonnet aux Bouillons

Bonnet à la paysanne d'un nouveau gout

27

PLATE 27

French Coiffures for 1776, engraved by Jacques Esnaut and Michel Rapilly for their *3ᵉ Cahier de Modes francaises pour les Coiffures depuis 1776*. Numerous plates for headdresses were produced from the mid 1770s until the late 1780s. A certain allowance must be made for the fashionable distortion in the drawing, but they are still notably large and complex and a very important aspect of fashion. Hair began to be dressed higher in the late 1760s and the third quarter of the 18th century was one of the great ages of the professional hairdresser. Well known practitioners of the time, like Stewart and Le Gros, published instruction books showing how the hair could be frizzed (backcombed), curled and mounted over pads. Caps sometimes given a topical title were produced in great number and variety by the 'marchandes de modes' in France and the milliners in England, and were an important accessory.

24923.1

PLATE 28

French Court Dress, dated 1779 drawn by Pierre Thomas Le Clère, engraved by N. Dupin, a pirate copy by J. M. Will from the *27ième Cahier de costumes français 21ième suite d'habillements à la mode (Galerie des Modes)*. The plate shows a 'robe de Demi Gala' of 'Pekin' (a type of silk) in the newest colour 'prune de Monsieur' slightly different from the hitherto fashionable 'puce' shade. The lady is said to be unusual in wearing diamond earrings and her floral spray is etiquette for her court rôle. The 'ecuyer' (equerry) wears a 'habit de demi-gala' embroidered only at the edges: full gala dress would have gold and silver embroidery throughout. His wig is 'en herisson' (hedgehog) and he has a plumed 'chapeau bras', to be carried not worn. He also has white gloves and red heels to his shoes, obligatory at court. Either he – or the engraver – has forgotten the sword knot.

French court etiquette was very strict and for the ladies prescribed a stiff boned bodice with ruffled sleeve bands and a train from the waist, archaic in style and recalling the fashions of the 1660s (PLATE 12). The dress is said to have been almost intolerably uncomfortable.

These elaborate dresses were the speciality of the French Marchandes des Modes. The best known, or most notorious, was Rose Bertin (1744–1813) who from her close association with Marie Antoinette was known as her 'Ministre des Modes'.

E.21595–1957

Jeune Dame qui quête: elle est vêtue d'une robe de Cour, de Pekin, garnie de gaze entrelassée de rubans et de guirlandes de fleurs. Celui qui la conduit est vêtu d'un habit de Gros de Naples, brodé autour en pailletes de toutes coul.rs

A. Augsbourg chez F. M. Will. Fauxbourg S. Jacques.

PLATE 29

Fashionable French outdoor dress, shown in *Le Rendez-vous pour Marly*, dated 1777, drawn by Jean Michel Moreau called 'Le Jeune' (1741–1814), and engraved by Carl Güttenburg for the second *Suite d'Estampes pour Servir à l'Histoire des Moeurs et du Costume des Français dans le Dix Huitième Siècle* . . . 1778.

26

30

31

PLATE 29 *continued*

The ladies wear the 'Polonaise', short with draped and gathered skirt. The petticoats, supported on small side-hoops, are ankle length and show the high heeled shoes. Though extremely chic, they were informal dress and it is instructive to compare them with the more formal trailing gowns worn by the ladies in the distance. The hair is dressed high (see PLATE 27). The parasol was an accessory whose popularity had been revived in the third quarter of the century after a lapse of fifty years. The gentleman's coat has a deep turn-down collar and double-breasted fastening. It is a country style only acceptable in town in the third quarter of the century. Colouring is muted. The children wear the simple less restrictive clothes introduced as healthier and more suitable for their active and growing bodies in accordance with the theories set out by Jean-Jacques Rousseau in *Emile*, 1763. The little boy is in what the French fashion journals called a sailor suit.   A.L.436–1890

PLATES 30, 31

Fashionable French Dress, anonymous engravings, probably from the *Cabinet des Modes*, 1787.

After 1785 the ladies' dresses become much more high waisted, with 'buffons' and puffed neckerchiefs to enlarge the bust and bustles and sashes to emphasise the behind. Sleeves tend to be narrow and wrist rather than elbow length. Large accessories like hats and muffs contrast with the trim silhouette. Men's coats become shorter and tighter, their slenderness emphasized by a preference for vertical striped fabrics, high collars and large cravats. Buttons, buckles and fobs are popular trimmings. The hat, brim folded fore and aft, not into a triangle, assumes a new outline.

(30) E.989–1959   (31) E.980–1959

Published as the Act directs May 1. 1796. by N. Heideloff. at the Gallery of Fashion Office N.º 90. Wardour Street.

PLATE 32

English Fashions, dated 1796, aquatint coloured by hand, by Niklaus Wilhelm Innocentius von Heideloff (1761–1837), in his *Gallery of Fashion*.

During the late 1780s and early 1790s, classical influences strengthen and the silhouette becomes straighter and shorter waisted. There is still emphasis at the bust but less padding at the hips. Fashions are still transitional.

The illustration 'Evening dresses for opera and concerts' confirms the arrival of the 'classical' shape, more or less natural, unconfined by corsets and unexaggerated by

padding. The waist line is just below the bust. Colours are pale and fabrics soft and flowing to suggest classical drapery, but the floating and concealing drapes of these English ladies suggest that they are uncertain about the propriety of too much paganism. Hair-styles are shorter and relatively unimportant by 1796.

This plate illustrates Heideloff's talent in grouping his figures and making use of minimum props to suggest a suitable scene to enhance the dresses.
Library

EVENING DRESS

PLATE 33

English dress, dated 1806, drawn by Devis, probably Arthur William Devis (1763–1822) and engraved by James Mitan (1776–1822) for *La Belle Assemblée*.

John Bell, the discriminating London publisher, has assembled artists of quality to do justice to this day and evening dress designed by Madame Lanchester, Bond Street dressmaker and francophile, able to emulate Parisian simplicity and purvey it to an English clientele. She was very publicity-conscious and her designs are to be found in most English ladies' journals, including the *Miroir de la Mode* which she herself published in 1803–6.
E.2477–1888

PLATE 34

English evening dress, dated 1824, anonymous engraving from *Ackermann's Repository of the Arts*.

French and English styles are in close accord. After *c.* 1818 the waist moved steadily lower to its natural level, and the sleeves became larger. The skirts have a wedge-shaped outline, smooth at the hips and flared at the hem, which is emphasized with trimmings.
Library.

Le Billet doux.

PLATE 35
French day dress, dated 'Floreal an.8' (1801), *Le Billet Doux*, drawn and engraved by Philippe Louis Debucourt (1755–1832) for *Modes et Manières du Jour à Paris à la Fin du 18ᵉ Siècle et au Commencement du 19ᵉ*, here illustrating 'Cheveux Retrousses', hair braided into a knot, and a waist-length 'Spencer de Velours', a style which *Costumes Parisiens* of 1798 ascribes to Lord Spencer's accident with his clothes. Simple light high-waisted dresses, short jackets and neat semiclassical hairstyles were ubiquitous among the fashionable and not so fashionable for the next two decades. Debucourt's elegant gentle narrative style is the model for the fashion plate artists of the early 20th century.
E.1158–1974

Paris. Merveilleuse. W.16.

Chapeau de paille d'Italie, par-dessus à la Chinoise.

36

Paris day dress, *c.* 1815, drawn by Horace Vernet (1789–1863) and engraved by Georges-Jacques Gatine (1773–after 1824) from the set published by Pierre La Mésangère, *Incroyables et Merveilleuses*. The title of the set recalls the plates by Carle Vernet, Horace Vernet's father, who caricatured the 'smart young things' of the Directoire when the terms were first used.

PLATE 36. The first English visitors after the defeat of Napoleon were delighted to be charmed and persuaded by the French fashion of dress, much more elaborately trimmed and with higher waists and fuller skirts than were worn on this side of the Channel.

PLATES 37, 38. The young men are more Dandy, in the contemporary tradition of George 'Beau' Brummell and the Prince Regent, than 'Incroyables' of the previous generation. Fortunes were spent at tailors perfecting the fit of their clothes and hours adjusting the lie and stiffness of their neckcloths. The coats with the squared-off cutaway tails are rationalised versions of the high-waisted styles of the Directoire and plain coloured wool rather than silk was now worn for day. Their sleeves, like those

Paris. Incroyable. N.° 5.

Chevelure à la François I.er. Chapeau en Barque. Charivari de Boulogne.

38

Paris. Incroyable. N.° 5.

Chapeau à la Robinson. Cheveux à l'Enfant. Pantalon de Tricot. Bottes à la Hussarde.

37

of the ladies, are cut full at the shoulders. Form-fitting 'pantaloons' (often made from jersey for extra 'cling') and trousers are conventional for informal day wear and breeches for formal occasions. Much attention is devoted to the fit of the nethergarments and they are hardly recognisable as the baggy working trousers of the 'sans culottes', labourer vanguards of the revolution. Hair has been worn short since the classical styles of the 1790s but the carefully curled 'coiffure François Iier' here looks forward to the systematically dishevelled locks of the Romantics. Hats worn with walking outfits such as these have crowns and brims; a carried 'chapeau bras' is used with formal clothes. The high crowned hat 'à la Robinson', the top hat of the next generation, may be named after the then fashionable Parisian resort 'Plessis-Robinson'.

(36) E.133–1947
(37) E.98–1947
(38) E.96–1947

PLATE 39
Anglo–French fashions. This anonymous engraving, dated January 1831, shows the sleeve steadily more bouffant since the mid 1820s and the elaborate hairstyles piled in interlinked braids. English and French fashions are now so close that *La Belle Assemblée* can re-engrave, not very well, two of the prints from Achille-Jacques Jean Marie Deveria's (1800–1857) series *Dix-Huit Heures de la Journée de la Parisienne, circa* 1830, and without acknowledging their origin publish *Dix Heures du Matin* and *Huit Heures du Soir* as French fashions suitable for English ladies. The morning dress is said to have been made from green 'gros des Indes' and the upper part of the sleeve is noted as being 'excessively large'. The bonnet is of canary yellow 'peluche' and the scarf is Kashmir. The evening dress is of velvet trimmed with 'blonde' lace and has 'beret' sleeves and a 'corsage à la Sevigné'.
E.1035–1959

PLATE 40
English fashions for 1832–3, an anonymous watercolour possibly an original for one of B. Read's fashion plate engravings. It shows clothes of the day by the Round Pond in Kensington Gardens. These are the first fashion

plates in which as much attention is paid to the backgrounds as to the clothes. The silhouette is similar for both men and women, with sleeves at their widest and waists long and tight. Skirts are ankle length, and materials light with many floral printed patterns. Hats and caps of various kinds are important accessories. They are much trimmed and have wide face-framing brims. The men wear formal dress coats with cutaway tails and less formal frock coats. The top hat is universal. The parasols are a curving 'pagoda' shape, recalling the Chinoiserie architectural style of the period. B. Read published a series of fashions in topographical settings c. 1827–1840. He was a tailor and sold the plates together with the patterns for the clothes in the pictures for 7/- the set.

E.2291–1931

PLATE 41

Fashionable Dress, *circa* 1837, probably engraved after Sulpice Guillaume Chevalier, called Paul Gavarni (1804–1866) for *La Gazette des Salons, No. 119.*

After 1836–7 there was a swift deflation in sleeve size, which became as narrow as it had been broad. At the same time skirts lengthened to the instep for both formal and informal wear. Hair styles were simplified, though the 'top knot' did not shrink into the bun until around 1840. Quieter colours and less obtrusive trimmings made the clothes as demure as they had formerly been exuberant. The lady wears a dress made by Mme Eccheville of 'Stradella' fabric, a bonnet by Baudrant and an embroidered mantle of 'taffetas lustré'. Men's clothes are as studied and as finely finished as they had been in Regency times, and the 'redingote', made by M. Humann, follows the same trend towards a smoother, more gently curving silhouette. The hat is made by M. Gibus, later to patent the collapsible opera hat, and the hair arranged by M. Seligmann. All the establishments are of the highest class. Gavarni was one of the supreme designers of the fashion plate, but unfortunately his work is rare in English public collections.

Library

PLATE 42

Ladies' Outdoor dress, dated 30/xi/1844, drawn by Ange-Louis Janet-Lange (1815–1872), and engraved by L. Wolf for the *Cabinet de Lecture et le Voleur reunis.* There was to be little change during the decade, though the tight sleeves began to widen at the cuff; on one of the dresses this has already happened. The waists are long and well corsetted, the skirts full and floor length, and held out by a quantity of stiffening petticoats. Hairstyles are smooth and cover the ears, and a lady-like isolation from reality is achieved by a blinker-like bonnet (here credited to Mantoy) set straight on the head and completely shielding ears and profile.

Library

41

42

PLATE 43

Fashionables. Fashionable young French men, *circa* 1840; a lithograph by De Frey after Gavarni. A figure study rather than a fashion plate, but all the better for showing both the cut of the clothes and the way they fit – or do not fit – the body. The new art of photography will from this date provide comment on the reality of dress as opposed to the ideal of the fashion plate. The high cravat, the pantaloons strapped beneath the feet, and the contrasts of pattern and texture are features of male dress on both sides of the Channel. The very long overcoat and straight tall hat are typical of extreme French styling.

E.1657–1888

AD GOUBAUD et Cie Edrs Paris

J. Fournage Impr de la Harpe 55 Paris

Jules David del.

PLATE 44

Anglo–French Fashions, dated 1860, engraved after Jules David (1808–1892), for syndication by F. Goubaud and purchased for publication in the *Englishwoman's Domestic Magazine* of July 1860. They show a young girl's ball dress of white gauze, wide sleeved and skirted, and an afternoon or visiting dress of purple striped silk (perhaps dyed with one of the new aniline dyes), worn with a wide-brimmed bonnet, tipped away from the face. This was an age of expansion and experiment, and skirts of this width would need the support of the artificial crinoline, introduced in 1856. The sewing machine became widely available during the later 1850s, and in 1860 Samuel Beeton produced paper patterns to accompany his French fashion plates – the first publisher to do so. High fashion was now within the reach of all his readers.

Library

PLATE 45
Anglo–French Fashions, dated 1872, engraved after Isabelle Toudouze (1872–1925) for publication in *Le Follet*. This dinner and walking dress illustrates the change to a softer line consciously based on the fashions of the 1770s, with a feeling for paler colours, lighter fabrics, and frilly trimmings. Fullness begins to concentrate at the back of the skirt in the later 1860s, and the increasing accumulation of drape and trimming needs the support of crinolette or bustle. Hairstyling becomes more elaborate, and the simple knot of the 1860s is built up into an elaborate bun with the aid of numerous false plaits and switches. Hats tipped over the forehead replace the former bonnet, and higher heels alter the entire stance of the body. *Le Follet* was a quality magazine, but it should be noted that the merchants advertising below the plate and endorsing the garments are *confection*, ready-to-wear and exporters, not the Haute Couture. Isabelle Toudouze, like the rest of her family, was adept at suggesting backgrounds suitable for showing off the clothes.
Library

REVUE DE LA MODE

PLATE 46
Anglo-French Fashions, dated 1877. Engraved after François Chiffrant (1825–1901) for *La Revue de la Mode*, May 21st 1876. It shows the revealing draped styles fashionable between 1876, when the fullness of the skirt is first 'tied back' so tightly that it hampers the gait, and 1881–2, when the bustle returns to support the train. The bodice is almost corset-like in the way it moulds and reveals the figure. The discomfort and occasional indecency of such fashions stimulated the move towards dress reform.
Library

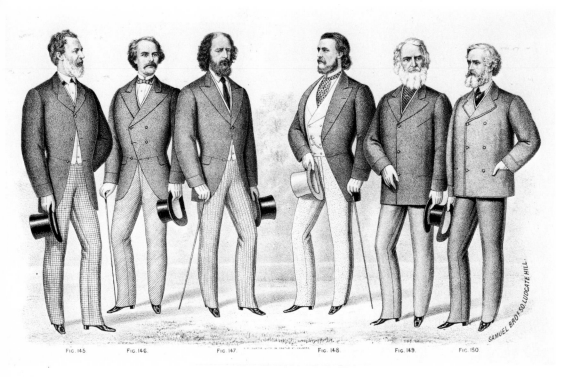

FIG. 145   FIG. 146.   FIG. 147.   FIG. 148.   FIG. 149.   FIG. 150

PLATE 47

English fashions for men: a lithograph by C. H. Curtis from the 1868 catalogue of Samuel Brothers, Merchant Tailors, Ludgate Hill (a City of London firm of mass-producing clothiers), entitled *Illustrative Portrait Groups, Princes Poets and Painters . . . represent the most fashionable and becoming attire for gentlemen and their sons.*

The heads are recognisable likenesses, copies from portrait photographs, though it is to be doubted whether the celebrities wore the clothes or were necessarily consulted at all. Prices ranged from about £2–£4.50. Fig. 145, Robert Browning wears a 'Professional Oxonian Suit', Fig. 146, Nathaniel Hawthorne – a 'Double Breasted morning suit', Fig. 147, Alfred Tennyson Esq., – a Cambridge suit', Fig. 148, Gerald Massey– the 'Dress Oxonian',

Fig. 149, Henry Wadsworth Longfellow – the 'Negligee suit', Fig. 150, Martin Farquehar Tupper – the 'Yachting suit'.

Big tailoring firms of this kind, producing large quantities of cheap clothing, tended to be associated with the notorious 'sweating' method of production. The suits sold, in line with the trend of the decade and intended for the artisan and lower middle classes, are comfortable and easy fitting, though possibly not too hard wearing. In the last quarter of the century, the 'negligee suit', the ancestor of the lounge suit, will become acceptable for most ordinary occasions, but in the mid 1860s it was still necessary to wear the frock or morning coat.

Library

48

49

PLATES 48, 49

Anglo–French evening and day dress, dated 1890 and 1895, engraved after Adolphe Charles Sandoz (1845–after 1925) for *The Queen*. PLATE 48, dated January 4th 1890 showing ball, dinner and evening gowns, illustrates the fashionable line in its mid point of change between the back emphasis of the bustle re-introduced by 1885, there-after becoming less important while sleeves grow in size.

PLATE 49, dated August 8th 1895: country, casino and travelling dresses have the new sleeve fully developed; after 1895 it slowly begins to shrink. The skirts flare smoothly from waist to feet and only a hint of back full-ness remains. The coat and skirt worn by the figure stand-ing in the foreground are garments which will become a basic part of most average women's wardrobes for the next half century.

The hats are made by Virot, the best known of the Paris milliners in the last quarter of the nineteenth century. The clothes are made by Worth, the most celebrated of Paris couture houses, founded by the Englishman Charles Frederick Worth (1825–1895) in 1856. Sandoz drew most of the couture plates in *The Queen* at this time and was very skilled at suggesting a social background suitable to the clothes.

Library

PLATE 50

English evening dress, dated 1900, engraved by Georges Labadie Pilotell(e) (1844–1918) for *The Queen*, 15th December 1900.

It was made by Redmayne's of Bond Street and described as a 'Princess Gown composed of maize satin veiled with accordian pleated chiffon and draped with ivory tulle, richly embroidered with applique, fine Chantilly lace, chenille and studded with pailettes'. Pilotelle's busy sinuous style is admirably adapted to the slim curving lines, broken by overlays of soft and fragile trimmings, fashionable in the late 1890s and early 1900s.

Library

51

PLATES 51, 52

French evening dress, lineblock and coloured stencil prints. PLATE 51 by Paul Iribe (*circa* 1880–1935) for *Les Robes de Paul Poiret*, 1908. PLATE 52 by Georges Lepape (1887–1971) for *Les Choses de Paul Poiret*, 1911.

Poiret's revolutionary contributions to fashion were simple lines and brilliant colours. He commissioned the first of these new departures in fashion publicity, limited edition albums of examples from his collections, when he had been established for only four years. There are no captions and there is only the picture to tell *and* sell the story, which it does to considerable effect.
Library

52

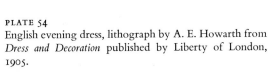

PLATE 53
French evening dress, *circa* 1912, drawing in pen and wash by Romain de Tirtoff (Erté) (1892).

A sketch made when he worked in Paul Poiret's studio 1912–13. All the large couture houses employed young designers who worked more or less anonymously helping to provide the large number of designs needed, and when necessary, sketch models to show to clients. This dress has a complex exotic quality which links it with Erté's later fashion and theatrical design.
E.570–1969

PLATE 54
English evening dress, lithograph by A. E. Howarth from *Dress and Decoration* published by Liberty of London, 1905.

An example of artistic or reform dress which Liberty had been providing ever since 1884 for clients who preferred timeless and comfortable garments to the fashionable norm. Liberty silks, supple, smooth and in unusual colour ranges, were specially suited to the style. In addition they sold furniture, silver and pottery by advanced designers – in short, a life style for the respectably artistic. Both Poiret and Liberty were in reaction to the overloaded fussiness of conventional taste. The catalogues are almost contemporary, but how different the solution; the English retreat into arts and crafts, the French into the exotic! Library

Robes pour l'été 1920.

55

PLATE 55

French fashions, lithograph by Raoul Dufy (1877–1953) in the *Gazette du Bon Ton No. 4*, May 1920, advertising fabrics by Bianchini-Ferrier.

The designers of the clothes are not mentioned. Fashions changed swiftly during the 1914–18 War, and from 1915–16 the principles of comfort and ease of movement were adopted by the majority of women, forced by the demands of the War effort to play an active rather than a passive role. In 1920 short, loose-fitting dresses were fashionable and though the length of the skirt and the waistline were to vary during the decade, a new norm had been established.

Circ 663–1968

PLATE 56

French fashions, a line block and coloured stencil by George Barbier published in *Art Gout et Beauté*, February 1922. The journal lists its artists but they do not sign their work, so this plate which shows the two most important fashion lines of the 1920s could have been by Marioton or Vittrotto, or Dory.

The girl standing beneath the tree wears an organdy dress by Lanvin (1867–1946), a couturière known for gently romantic full skirted 'robes de style' and for fine workmanship. The straight-cut low-waisted dress is by Doucet, still a prestige house, though no longer so important as in the late 19th century. For all its simple lines, it is a masterpiece of understated luxury. A slender boyish figure has replaced the rounded curve of the 'Belle Epoque' lady.

Library

PLATE 57

Anglo–French fashions, drawn by René Bouet–Willaumez for *Vogue*, December 24th 1937. These informal smart day clothes have the square shoulder line characteristic of the second half of the 1930s and popularised by the Italo–French couturière Elsa Schiaparelli (1890–1972) which were to remain in fashion until the New Look of 1947. Hats were an important accessory in the 1930s and these, tipped forward over the eyes, are typical. The crepe toque is designed by Agnes, the famous French modiste. The coat is inexpensive but effective fur. Similar clothes to these were to remain fashionable through World War II. Eric and Bouet-Willaumez were regarded by *Vogue* as rivals.

Library

White organdy dress with patterns of English embroidery, over-embroidered with red cotton.
Jeanne Lanvin

Pink Georgine crepe afternoon dress, trimmed with rose petals.
Doucet

56

57

Chanel dines at home
in printed pyjamas,
sweater, barbaric jewels.
(Two small Chanels)
Striped linen flannel jacket
Checked tussin, chiffon capeveil.

PLATE 58
French fashions, dated 1937, gouache by Christian Bérard (1902–49) reproduced in *Vogue*, July 7th, 1937, of clothes designed and worn by Gabrielle Chanel (1883–1971) the designer most representative of the trends of post-World War I fashion. For evening she promoted romantic colourful styles and for day easy fitting supple suits. She was among the first to bring back the trouser suit, here seen in evening version, considered almost as shocking in the 1930s as Paul Poiret's harem skirt-cum-trousers in the 1900s. Bérard summarises all the characteristics of her designs in this one plate.
Library

PLATE 59
French fashions, gouache by Christian Bérard (1902–49) reproduced in *Vogue*, October 19th 1938, of evening fashions designed by Elsa Schiaparelli the couture designer with whose sense of colour and fantasy Bérard was perhaps in greatest sympathy. He is said to have inspired the embroidery design of the 'Roi soleil' sunburst embroidered on the shocking pink (essentially Schiaparelli's colour) of the central cloak. A broad shouldered silhouette with slender skirt was typical of the later 1930s and early 1940s. *Vogue* comments on 'Schiaparelli's sky bright colours . . . Aerostatic purple, cameo pink, Uranus yellow' and the plate is a credit to the extraordinarily high standard of their pre-war colour printing.
Library

PLATE 60

Anglo–French evening dress, drawn by Carl Erickson
(Eric) reproduced in *Vogue*, October 19th 1938. The formal
evening dresses are by Paris couturières: that in the foreground is by Alix and the other by Lanvin. They are
decolleté and bouffant in the retrospective romantic style
of 1936–9. It had replaced the slimmer bias-cut line typical
of the later 1920s and early 1930s.
Library

Bibliography & Sources

Illustrations of dress and fashion have been acquired by the Victoria and Albert Museum as part of its service to art and design since it was founded in 1851. The collection is now one of the most comprehensive in the world and is distributed through several Departments. The main series is in the Department of Prints, Drawings and Photographs, which collaborates with the Twentieth Century Archive in collecting documentation on the work of modern designers. The Archive shares with the National Art Library the accumulation of Trade catalogues. This Library has always been consciously comprehensive in its selection of books on contemporary and historical dress though not on the anthropological or ethnographic aspects. It contains an important series of early illustrated books (*Trachtenbücher*) and technical works on tailoring and cutting. The ever growing series of periodicals, which includes most of the main fashion journals from the 18th century to the present day, contains many fashion plates still associated with their original explanatory texts. The clothes themselves, textiles, pattern books and fashion dolls are to be found in the Department of Textiles and Dress and add an essential extra dimension. Theatrical costume is the responsibility of the Theatre Museum. There is no single printed catalogue or reference to fashion and dress illustration, but there are ongoing subject and artist indices in the Department of Prints, Drawings and Photographs, and a similar subject and author catalogue in the National Art Library.

No single book covers fashion illustration between the 16th and 20th centuries. The most readily available secondary works are more concerned with the later periods; V. Holland, *Hand Coloured Fashion Plates 1770–1899*, London 1955, and D. Langley Moore, *Fashion through Fashion Plates 1771–1970*, London 1965, are general surveys, the latter more detailed on the late 18th century while the former contains a useful summary list of 19th century fashion plate artists. S. Sitwell, *Gallery of Fashion*, 1969, gives new insight into English and French fashion plates of the 18th and early 19th centuries. M. Battersby, *Art Deco Fashions; French Designers 1908 to 1925*, London 1974, and J. Robinson, *The Golden Age of Style*, London 1977, deal specifically with the 20th century. J. Robinson's is the more detailed with a useful section on the *pochoir* process and it has a good source list. James Laver's *Fashion and Fashion Plates*, 1943, is a sound though brief introduction.

More detailed information is to be found in exhibition catalogues: Paris, Louvre, Cabinet Edmund de Rothschild, *Modes et Costume Français 1574–1815*, Paris 1966, concentrates on French sources; Rotterdam, Museum Boijmans van Beuningen, *Von Wambuis tot Frac: het Kostuum in de Prentkunst circa 1450 – circa 1800*, 1977, and also *Het Kostuum in de Prentkunst*, 1977, on Netherlands engravers; London, The Costume Society, *From Hollar to Heideloff*, 1979, is a good introduction to the whole subject of dress and fashion illustration from the 16th to the early 19th century giving particular emphasis to artists working in England. The Scottish Arts Council and the Victoria and Albert Museum, *Fashion 1900–1939*, sets fashion and its illustration in the artistic context of the 20th century. Paris, Galeries de Luxembourg, *Illustrateurs des Modes et Manières en 1925*, 1972, is somewhat slight but provides a listing of artists of the 'art deco' period.

Some of the most useful contributions can only be found in periodicals. The *Trachtenbücher* receive their clearest and most systematic treatment to date in J. Olian, *Sixteenth Century Costume Books, Dress Vol.3.*, Costume Society of America, 1977. They are also mentioned in J. L. Nevinson's authoritative general survey of the 16th to 18th centuries, *The Origin of the Fashion Plate*, Centro Internazionale delle Arte e del Costume, 1952/1955, and in *The Origin and Early History of the Fashion Plate*, Smithsonian Press, Washington, 1969. He concentrates on French late 17th century fashion journalism in 'The Mercury Gallant or European Fashions in the 1670s', *Connoisseur*, Vol. CXXXVI, 1955, and 'Fashion plates and fashion, 1625–1635,' *Apollo*, Vol. LI, 1950.

There is no shortage of copiously illustrated and facsimile editions which often have excellent introductions, notably P. Cornu's to the 13 vol. series, *Documents pour l'histoire du Costume*, and to reprints of the *Galeries des Modes 1778–1787*, 5 vols, Paris 1911 to 1914. Further selections from French fashion plates will be found in *Costumes et Moeurs d'autrefois*, vols I–VII, Editions Rombaldi, edited R. A. Weigert, though these are mainly useful for their pictorial content: *Incroyables et Merveilleuses*, 1955, *Galeries des Modes et Costumes Français*, 1956, *Bonnart; personnages de Qualité 1680–1715*, 1956, *Modes et Manières du jour à Paris*, 1957, *Pourpoints et Vertugadins*, 1958, and the final volume, ed. F. L. L. Boucher, *Paris Miroir de la Mode*, 1959. The Costume Society (Hon. Sec.

Mrs A. Thomas, 251 Popes Lane, London W3) has issued facsimile editions of significant English works with brief but sound introductions; B. Lens, *The Exact Dress of the Head 1725*, Extra Series 2, 1970; H. Moses, *Designs of Modern Costume 1812*, Extra Series 4, 1973; W. Hollar, *The Four Seasons*, Extra Series 6, 1979.

Dover Books, New York, have published selections from C. Vecellio, *A Renaissance Costume Book*, 1975, and S. Blum provides brief introductions to *Victorian Fashions and Costumes from Harpers Bazaar 1867–1898*, 1974, and to R. Ackermann, *Costume Plates; Women's Fashion in England 1818–1828*, 1979. For London, Victoria and Albert Museum, J. Laver edited a Large Picture Book *Costume Illustration of the Seventeenth and Eighteenth Centuries*, 1951, and C. Gibbs Smith used English and French plates to provide a five yearly survey of fashions in the nineteenth century in *The Fashionable Lady in the Nineteenth Century*.

Despite this generous coverage, fashion plates gain much from being considered in their artistic context. The more important artists attract monographs but the others can only be found, and then not invariably, in the most exhaustive biographical dictionaries. It is extremely un-

fortunate that the authoritative Paris, Bibliothèque Nationale, *Fonds Français* covering the sixteenth to twentieth centuries, is incomplete and does not yet include any artist whose name initial is to be found in the second part of the alphabet.

The journalistic and literary aspects are treated in A. Adburgham, *Women in Print, writing women and women's magazines from the Restoration to the accession of Queen Victoria*, London, 1974, and in G. White, *Women's magazines*, London, 1964.

Books on the fashion background are too numerous to list but J. Colas, *Bibliographie Générale du Costume et de la Mode*, 2 vols., Paris, 1933, and F. J. Lipperheide, *Katalog der Freiherrlich von Lipperheideschen Kostumbibliothek*, 2 vols., Berlin, 1905, new ed., 1965, are essential guides to primary and secondary sources. London, The Costume Society, *Costume, a bibliography*, 2nd ed., 1974, lists the more easily available works but for the twentieth century should be supplemented with memoirs by magazine editors and illustrators, *inter alia*, E. Woolman Chase and I. Chase, *Always in Vogue*, 1954, Bettina Ballard, *In my Fashion*, London 1964 and Cecil Beaton's pictorial surveys of the period and his autobiography.